JONATHAN LICHTENSTEIN

Jonathan Lichtenstein's previous work includes *Station*, premiered at the Soho Theatre, London, in 2000, directed by Abigail Morris, and two radio plays: *Moving the Scrolls* (BBC Radio Four, 2000), also directed by Abigail Morris, and *Human Rights* (BBC Radio Four, 2001, repeated on BBC Radio Seven, 2004), directed by Jeremy Mortimer. Jonathan Lichtenstein is the Director of the Centre for Theatre Studies at the University of Essex.

Other Titles in this Series

Jonathan Lichtenstein

THE PULL OF NEGATIVE GRAVITY

NICK HERN BOOKS
London
www.nickhernbooks.co.uk

A Nick Hern Book

The Pull of Negative Gravity first published in Great Britain
as a paperback original in 2004 by Nick Hern Books Limited,
14 Larden Road, London W3 7ST

The Pull of Negative Gravity copyright © 2004
Jonathan Lichtenstein

Jonathan Lichtenstein has asserted his right to be identified
as the author of this work

Cover image: © Digital Vision / Creatas

Typeset by Country Setting, Kingsdown, Kent CT14 8ES
Printed and bound in Great Britain by Cox and Wyman Ltd,
Reading, Berks

A CIP catalogue record for this book is available from
the British Library

ISBN 1 85459 839 2

For Barbara

The Pull of Negative Gravity was first performed by the Mercury Theatre Company at the Traverse Theatre, Edinburgh, on 5 August 2004 and subsequently at the Mercury Theatre, Colchester. The cast was as follows:

BETHAN	Louise Collins
VI	Joanne Howarth
DAI	Daniel Hawksford
RHYS	Lee Haven-Jones

Director   Gregory Thompson
Designer   Ellen Cairns
Lighting Designer   Robin Carter
Sound Designer   Andrea J Cox
Movement Director   Nicola Rosewarne
Script Editor   Barbara Peirson

The play was previously read at the National Theatre Studio, London, on 26 January 2004 with the following cast:

BETHAN	Mali Harries
VI	Barbara Peirson
DAI	Matt Ryan
RHYS	Lee Haven-Jones

Director   Simon Usher

THE PULL OF NEGATIVE GRAVITY

Jonathan Lichtenstein

Characters

BETHAN

DAI

RHYS

VI

Prologue

A tin of stones

VI *enters and picks out a stone from a cake tin. She holds it up to the light. It has a hole in it. She puts it into her mouth and holds it there for a moment. She removes the stone and puts it back in the tin.*

Scene One

Bethan dances on the hill

The top of a hill in Wales.

Early morning. Summer.

BETHAN *is dancing slowly. We hear the noise of a Chinook helicopter approaching. It passes low, overhead, deafening.* BETHAN *looks up. She raises her hands. For a moment she is dancing with the Chinook as the down force blows her about.*

Scene Two

Vi stuffs the envelopes, Bethan avoids the hospital

The kitchen of a small farmhouse.

The same morning.

VI *is stuffing envelopes.*

BETHAN. I was on the hill.

VI. Again?

BETHAN. Did you hear it?

VI. Horrible thing.

BETHAN. It was circling.

VI. Sounded like it went straight over to me.

BETHAN. No, no, it circled.

VI. Bethan, please.

BETHAN. You heard it. It's him. He circled round the hill.

VI. You've told me this a thousand times.

BETHAN. Like he promised he would.

VI. It went straight to the hospital.

BETHAN. It circled.

VI. It's the burns run. If anyone should know that it's you . . .

BETHAN. This one was so low I saw the heat from the engines.

VI. It was preparing to land at the hospital. They'll be calling for you in a minute. Pass me that box, will you? They use the hill as a visual marker.

BETHAN *passes the box.*

BETHAN. It went round the hill.

VI. They go as low as they do for devilment. I've said this so many times before.

BETHAN. It looked ancient, like a dinosaur.

VI. So you keep saying. You get too close, my girl. You better watch out, those blithering things can be dangerous. There's an accident waiting to happen if you ask me.

BETHAN *lifts up an envelope.*

BETHAN. What do you earn from these?

VI. Every little counts.

BETHAN. You should do something else.

VI. Like what?

BETHAN. I don't know.

VI. Cadw'r blaidd o'r drws.

BETHAN. What?

VI. Keeps the wolf from the door.

BETHAN. It's a lot of time.

VI. Do you think I'd do it if I didn't have to?

BETHAN. It's not normal, is it?

VI. What?

BETHAN. It's not right.

VI. It's unusual.

BETHAN. It's deranged. I know. I can't help it. It's an
    addiction. A sore, a cut, a bruise. It helps. Can't work today.

VI. You have to work.

BETHAN. I won't. Not today.

VI. You're better when you work.

BETHAN. Not today. Not work.

VI. You're not staying in my kitchen, brooding. I've got this lot
    to finish by tomorrow.

BETHAN. Something's happening to me.

VI. Pull yourself together.

BETHAN. I'm falling.

VI. Stop it!

BETHAN. Hold me. Hold me. Please.

    VI *holds* BETHAN.

VI. It's not much.

BETHAN. Tight.

VI. I wish I could make you happy.

They hold each other. DAI *dances through the kitchen.*

BETHAN. Dai!

VI. Don't do that.

BETHAN. I see him.

VI. He'll be back.

BETHAN. I feel sick.

VI. I'm sure he'll come back.

BETHAN. Maybe. I waved at the pilot. He waved at me.

VI. Of course he did.

BETHAN. They get so close when I dance with them.

VI. Bethan.

BETHAN. And the colours of the grass and the sky and the clouds and everything's magnified and I go somewhere else and I'm full up and I'm touching space and I'm close to the me of me.

VI. For God's sake!

BETHAN. Like I don't exist.

VI. Stop it. It's not right.

BETHAN. You miss him, don't you?

VI. I miss him all the time. It should've been Rhys who went. The army might have knocked some sense into him. Then this farm might not be in such a predicament. And if Dai had stayed instead of him you'd have been walked down that aisle a beaming girl.

BETHAN. I meant Gwilym.

VI. Gwilym?

BETHAN. You miss him.

VI. His absence fills me.

BETHAN. You're crying.

VI. No I'm not.

BETHAN. Why're you so tough?

VI. You want me to mope, don't you?

BETHAN. No.

VI. That sort of behaviour does no one any good.

BETHAN. Why were you so hard after his funeral?

VI. I was sensible.

BETHAN. You were like a fox.

VI. Everything had to be sorted. Someone had to do it. Farms
    don't manage themselves. Not one of you was capable. All
    of you were crying and pulling your hair out.

BETHAN. You fished him out of the river.

VI. I did.

BETHAN. Early that morning.

VI. Yes.

BETHAN. Your drowned husband.

VI. Yes.

BETHAN. How did he look?

VI. How did he look? Wet.

Flashback: VI's *memory of Gwilym's wake.* DAI *and* RHYS
enter. DAI *hugs* VI *then* BETHAN. RHYS *moves to* VI.

RHYS. It was a good turnout.

VI. No more than you'd expect.

RHYS. Half the village, I'd say. The vicar gave a good speech.

DAI. Does a good funeral does Reverend Hughes.

RHYS *and* DAI *hold each other.*

I wish he was still here.

RHYS. Me too.

DAI. Still can't believe it.

RHYS. Nor me.

DAI. I keep thinking he'll walk through that door.

RHYS. All those bloody fights. Now all I want is to see him again.

DAI. Stupid old man.

RHYS. Funny thing is I can't really remember what we argued about.

DAI. You argued about everything.

RHYS. You were just as bad.

DAI. Me?

RHYS. Yes, you.

DAI. Perhaps.

RHYS. Hutchison was there. He's put on a bit of weight.

DAI. It's prosperity must do that to you.

VI. Blinking boy swum all the way from Cardiff.

DAI. Don't start, Mother.

VI. You don't have to have a fin on your back to be a shark. He was sniffing round like a dog.

DAI. Please, not now.

VI. Paul Hutchison. Coming like that, dressed in black.

DAI. He came to pay his respects.

VI. Wretched thing.

DAI. Father knew him when he was a lad. He was upset.

VI. I'm sorry to hear of your loss, he says, and if you need any help financially, the London purchasers are still interested, then he pauses. Mind you, they're not aware of the specifics as yet. And who's going to blinking tell 'em, I said.

DAI. They'd offered a fair price.

VI. A fair price? What's fair about it? Tell me that. What's the price of history? Of family?

DAI. The market price.

VI. The market price, the sale's off. I've told him.

DAI. What do you mean you've told him?

VI. I've told him. It's off.

DAI. You mustn't do that. How many times have we been through this?

VI. Us Williamses have been here for generations and sometimes there's hardship and sometimes there's plenty and they run into each other. And now we're holding the farm together, until better times. Boys. We always said. We just need a breathing space. You could sort it out. Just for a year or two. Surely. Rhys? Dai?

They don't reply.

Put out the sherry, Bethan.

BETHAN *pours the sherry.*

A toast.

They raise their glasses.

To my dear departed husband. My Gwilym.

BETHAN. Gwilym.

RHYS. To Father.

DAI. Father.

VI. I bloody loved you, Gwilym. I bloody loved you!

They drink.

Another one. Raise your glasses. To Llanelwedd Farm.

BETHAN. Llanelwedd.

DAI. No.

VI. Come on, boys.

RHYS. Llanelwedd.

VI. Dai.

DAI. No.

VI. You must do it.

DAI. I don't want to. I've told you we have to sell the farm. We've got an offer and we have to leave.

VI. It's his funeral. Make the toast.

DAI. We've got an offer.

VI. Do it, please.

DAI. Mother.

VI. I said.

DAI. Why should I?

VI. For his memory and our future. Llanelwedd. It's his funeral.

They wait.

DAI. Llanelwedd.

VI. Done.

DAI. If you say so.

VI. I do.

The memory of the wake dissolves as BETHAN*'s bleeper sounds.*

BETHAN. The bloody burnt and the bloody dying.

VI. Work's good for you.

BETHAN. Work's killing me.

VI. It's healing you.

BETHAN. They'll have to manage without me.

VI. Pull yourself together. Bring me another couple of boxes, will you?

BETHAN *gets two more boxes.*

BETHAN. How many of these things do you have? The room's completely full.

VI. Never mind that, just put them by the table.

BETHAN. Can I help?

VI. Yes. Go to work.

BETHAN. When they're badly burnt, they piss out of a little tube.

VI. Do they?

BETHAN. They scream.

VI. Perhaps we should go away on a holiday.

BETHAN. You think as you see them in such pain, how can this be?

VI. Listen to me.

BETHAN. Some of them. Their cocks are burnt off . . . did you know that?

VI. No. I didn't.

BETHAN. I take a swab from their mouth, so that they can do the DNA test to work out who it is lying there in the bed in front of me. They're so burnt that no one knows for sure who they are.

VI. Why is the hospital up here?

BETHAN. The air's cooler so it helps their skin feel soothed. If you're seriously burnt, your skin feels like it's still on fire.

VI. I must take you away.

BETHAN. Where?

VI. We'll go somewhere really beautiful.

BETHAN. I want him to walk into this room.

VI. I'll get holiday brochures.

BETHAN. I want him to lift me into the air, hold my hand, cradle my head; like he did.

VI. I'll take you to Cardiff. We'll go shopping, buy clothes, it'll take your mind off things.

BETHAN. And just how are you going to pay for that?

VI. When I've finished stuffing all these.

BETHAN. Who are they for this time?

VI *holds up one of the cards.*

VI. Health insurance. It says you can win a fortune if you insure yourself.

BETHAN. You are a winner! Scratch and win £10,000! Match all six raspberries to win! Scratch off the silver geese to see if you take home our big money prize. It would be nice.

VI. Nice, it would be remarkable.

BETHAN *starts scratching a card.*

Don't do that.

BETHAN. You never know.

VI. They keep the winning cards separate.

BETHAN. What?

VI. The man who dropped them off told me.

BETHAN. I suppose they have to do that.

VI. This room would be full of scratched cards if they didn't.

BETHAN. All I want to do is wake up in the morning with him and touch his face.

VI. We need to go somewhere, somewhere different, somewhere away from all this. Then perhaps you'll stop all that dancing nonsense.

BETHAN*'s bleeper sounds again.*

You must go and you must help them.

BETHAN. I can't.

VI. You make them better.

BETHAN. Do I? I have love in me. I talk to them, try to hold them with my voice. I can do that. I know. Holding someone else with my words. But all they want to do is die.

The bleeper sounds.

Yesterday, one of them pulled all the tubes out of his body. I came in in the morning and I had to put them all back in. While he wept. It wasn't love that put them back. Real love would have been to leave him. Hold his hand. Let him be.

VI. Dying's a cop-out.

BETHAN. You think so? Sometimes I wonder.

VI. What?

BETHAN. If it's the thing we've all been searching for.

VI. Hold my hand.

BETHAN. I spend too much time here. I should go home, wash my clothes.

VI. You're more than welcome to stay, Bethan.

BETHAN. I feel closer to him here.

The bleeper sounds again. She switches it off.

VI. You mustn't switch it off.

BETHAN. I just did.

VI. You can't.

BETHAN. I have to.

VI. Your dancing.

BETHAN. I'll stop.

VI. Don't do that.

BETHAN. So you like it all of a sudden?

VI. Not exactly.

BETHAN. It's not normal.

VI. No, no, it's not but hold my hand. I don't . . .

BETHAN. Dance?

VI. Yes. That's right, I don't.

BETHAN. You want to dance, don't you?

VI. I'll drive you to your work. Look outside at the hedges, so
green and the honeysuckle, I planted that. You must go.
He'd want it. It's what he'd be proud of.

BETHAN. I'm not going.

VI. You've only got one life, you have to live it.

Scene Three

Hospital One: the burnt soldier

Hospital ward.

Day.

*The patient is covered in bandages in the hospital on a bed
connected to a heart monitor. BETHAN enters and takes a
swab from his mouth.*

BETHAN. It's a beautiful day out there. Really warm and easy.
Do you like birds? There's a new swallow's nest on the
back of the hospital. Really high on the eaves. I watched
them swooping through the air eating the insects. You know
if a swallow lands on the ground, it dies. It can't take off
again. It needs a ledge. Did you know that?

It'll be difficult for you now, there's no doubt about that. It's
uphill from here but everyone's ever so proud of you. You
know that, don't you?

You served your country in Iraq. And now you're here. For
better or for worse.

She checks his penis.

God.

BETHAN *leaves.*

The heart monitor remains bleeping constantly.

Scene Four

Bethan and Rhys

The hill.

Late afternoon.

RHYS *is on the hill gazing at the view.* BETHAN *climbs to the top.*

RHYS. Here again?

BETHAN. Yes. Been here long?

RHYS. No. Air's fresh.

BETHAN. Yes.

RHYS. Blowing from the Atlantic. Just finished your shift?

BETHAN. Yeah.

RHYS. Two thousand miles of fresh air. When it's this clear you can see Rhayader if you look over this way.

BETHAN. Can you?

RHYS. Never noticed 'til recently.

BETHAN. How far's that?

They stand and look.

RHYS. Twenty-five miles or so. Doesn't happen that often. Just when the air's breezing in.

See. There. Between those hills.

BETHAN. I can see it.

RHYS *flips a coin.*

RHYS. Heads or tails?

BETHAN. Heads.

RHYS. You win. Keep it.

BETHAN. No.

RHYS. Go on.

BETHAN. If it pleases you.

RHYS. I still come everyday.

BETHAN. I come when I can.

RHYS. Like we used to. I come every day.

BETHAN. It's your land.

RHYS. It's the family's, yes. I don't see you so much now.

BETHAN. I thought it best.

RHYS. You're probably right.

BETHAN. It's not easy.

RHYS. No. It's not. Haven't heard from him recently.

BETHAN. Me neither.

RHYS. And Vi too. She's heard nothing.

BETHAN. She said.

RHYS. She's worried sick.

BETHAN. She is. Yes.

RHYS. Something's happened to him.

BETHAN. We don't know.

RHYS. The things that go on there, that you hear on the news.
There are so many attacks every day. You'd think they'd be
pleased to have us there.

BETHAN. Please stop.

RHYS. It's frightening. I miss you.

BETHAN. No.

RHYS. So much.

BETHAN. I'm going.

RHYS. I won't touch you.

BETHAN. You do understand, don't you?

RHYS. Yes.

BETHAN. Thank you.

RHYS. That's OK.

BETHAN. I want to touch you but I can't.

RHYS. Good. I agree.

BETHAN. It wouldn't be proper.

RHYS. No. It wouldn't.

BETHAN. Not in that way.

RHYS. Can we just lie here together? As close friends.

BETHAN. Possibly.

RHYS. I fell in love with you the moment you walked into the room.

BETHAN. You said.

RHYS. Stupid.

BETHAN. It happens.

RHYS. I didn't speak to you for six months. Nerves. I never drink normally. Thought I'd impress. Spilt it all, all that drink all over you.

BETHAN. Pimm's.

RHYS. Horrible stuff. For Londoners really.

BETHAN. That was the evening Geraint Jones wore that huge banana costume.

RHYS. I love you.

BETHAN. He danced all night in it, didn't he?

RHYS. Yes and he sweated like a pig.

BETHAN. And then we all went to the river and he jumped in and then he got off with Myra Hughes and he asked her to marry him and he was dressed as a banana. A soaking wet banana.

RHYS. I love you so much.

BETHAN. God, I need to laugh. I need to laugh and laugh.

RHYS. I love you.

BETHAN. Help me.

RHYS. There's no one else.

BETHAN. I need help.

RHYS. I want you.

BETHAN. Please. Help. Help me.

RHYS. How?

BETHAN. Your hand. Like you used to.

RHYS. Are you sure you want me to?

BETHAN. If it's alright.

>BETHAN *lies down.* RHYS *places his hands on her head.*

>It's comforting.

RHYS. I feel stupid.

BETHAN. Don't.

RHYS. Can't help it.

BETHAN. It's what I want.

RHYS. I'll stroke your head.

BETHAN. Tell me good things.

RHYS. Like I used to?

BETHAN. Yes. Please. Like before.

RHYS. Sometimes I lie here when the wind drops in the
evening, when it's balanced between going out to the sea
and coming into the land. I feel it on my cheeks. One cheek
cool as the wind passes over it. Then stillness. Then the
wind changing and brushing on the other cheek. Like being
licked. I lie on the grass. I hear the air. And the sheep
bleating and the occasional dog barking, and the river down
in the valley and the clouds and the grass blowing.

BETHAN. Go on.

RHYS. Are you sure?

BETHAN. Please.

RHYS. I feel everything.

BETHAN. Go on.

RHYS. Everything breathes together, not separate, everything's
co-ordinated, everything within time, like time is treacle and
we're all in it, moment by moment. So the bird's wings
beating the air are occupying the same space as my breath,
and my ribs are moving in the same moment as clouds. And
then I can see everything in the world. The leaves in the
forests, swans on estuaries, mackerel in their shoals in the
deep sea. People going about their daily lives.

BETHAN. That's beautiful.

RHYS. And I'm fucking you.

BETHAN. No.

RHYS. Like we did.

BETHAN. These things happen.

RHYS. We're kissing and you're naked.

BETHAN. Please.

RHYS. We're talking. We're old. We're drinking tea quietly. At
home. In front of a fire. In winter.

BETHAN. I wish I loved you in the way you want me to.

RHYS. I get so confused.

BETHAN. Accept me.

RHYS. I love you.

BETHAN. I threw the rings in with him not you.

RHYS. I was there. It was nothing. A foolishness. Into the river. It could have been me.

BETHAN. You were beautiful that evening.

RHYS. We made love. We fucked. Why did you do that?

BETHAN. I can't explain everything. I don't know. I wanted to.

RHYS. You loved him more.

BETHAN. You must remember why it was.

RHYS. Must I?

BETHAN. It was an impulse. Perhaps I thought that if we fucked you would understand something; that I'm normal, that I'm the same as other girls.

RHYS. I loved it. I want more.

BETHAN. We fucked. It was no big deal. I've fucked quite a lot of people. It's normal.

RHYS. Don't say that.

BETHAN. I like to fuck.

RHYS. Please. Don't say that.

BETHAN. But I do.

RHYS. You joined those rings with him and then you threw them into the Ithon and then you made love with me. Just doesn't make sense.

BETHAN. These things don't.

RHYS. If he doesn't come back?

BETHAN. If he doesn't come back?

RHYS. It might happen.

BETHAN. He will come back.

RHYS. I could wait years for you.

BETHAN. When he comes home.

RHYS. What if he comes home in a body bag?

BETHAN. No.

RHYS. It's possible.

BETHAN. I'm clinging to him. His hands. His eyes. His mouth.

RHYS. Don't miss your chance with me, Bethan.

BETHAN. Here. Sit. Listen.

They listen to the wind.

RHYS. What?

BETHAN. Can you hear it?

RHYS. What?

BETHAN. Stand up! Feel it?

RHYS. What're you talking about?

BETHAN. In your legs. It comes up from the ground, through your legs. Feel it?

RHYS. No.

BETHAN. The vibration.

RHYS. I can't feel anything.

BETHAN. Chinooks. You feel them before you hear them, before you see them. Can you feel it now?

RHYS. I don't know.

BETHAN. It comes up from the ground, through into your feet, into your legs. Shut your eyes. Concentrate. Feel it. It's pushing up. Through your feet, up through your legs into your arse, into your cunt, into your belly, into your chest, into your head, into your brain. And out the other side.

BETHAN *begins to dance.*

Dance with me?

RHYS. I can't.

BETHAN. Dance!

RHYS. I don't want to.

BETHAN. Just do anything!

RHYS. I bloody can't.

BETHAN. Just try anything.

RHYS. I can't.

BETHAN. Just move, you'll be OK.

RHYS. I've forgotten how to.

BETHAN. It's coming out of me.

> *She laughs. The noise of the Chinook crescendoes.*
> BETHAN *dances. Then collapses.*

Scene Five

Rhys remembers the tossing of the coins (1)

By the river.

Evening.

DAI. Best of five.

RHYS. Best of twenty-one.

DAI. Best of thirteen.

RHYS. Best of seventeen.

DAI. Fifteen.

RHYS. Fifteen.

DAI. Shall we start?

RHYS. Why not?

DAI. Who goes first?

RHYS. I'll go first.

DAI. No way. I go first.

RHYS. Let's toss for it.

DAI. Alright.

RHYS. You toss, I'll call.

DAI. No, I'll call.

RHYS. No. I'll call.

DAI. Best of five?

RHYS. Best of five to decide who goes first and then best of fifteen.

DAI. Exactly.

Scene Six

Vi breaks the news

The kitchen.

The same evening.

VI *is lighting candles which cover the room.* RHYS *carries* BETHAN *in.*

RHYS. Bloody hell, it's like church in here.

VI. Is she alright?

RHYS. She was dancing on the hill. One of the Chinooks flew over and she keeled. She followed it with her eyes and leant back too far. Daft. She's heavy.

BETHAN. Hey!

RHYS. I had to carry her down the whole bloody hill.

VI. Are you alright, Bethan?

BETHAN. Feel a bit sick.

VI. Why don't you rest with us tonight?

BETHAN. Thanks.

VI. It's happened before. She'll feel better soon enough after a rest. Won't you, Bethan?

BETHAN. Yes. Thanks, Vi.

VI. Why don't you put her on the settee, Rhys.

RHYS. Where?

VI. On the settee. You go to sleep now.

BETHAN. Thanks.

VI. Sleep.

> BETHAN *sleeps in* RHYS*'s arms.*

> Put her down.

RHYS. You never light candles, what're you doing?

VI. I said put her down.

RHYS. She started shouting something but the helicopter was so deafening, I don't know what she said. It was so low I could smell it. She dances like a crazed bullock. So why all the candles?

VI. Put her down.

RHYS. What're they for?

VI. Put her down.

RHYS. I'll turn the lights on.

VI. Don't. I'm praying.

RHYS. What's happened?

VI. There's been an ambush. He's alright.

RHYS. He's alright?

VI. He's alright. He's alive.

RHYS. What's happened?

VI. I'll tell you in a minute when you've put her down.

RHYS. No.

VI. You're his brother.

RHYS. She fainted.

VI. You know what I mean.

RHYS. I'll put her on the settee.

He puts her on the settee.

VI. You're too close.

RHYS. We're just friends.

VI. You're his brother. How's he going to feel when he gets back?

RHYS. What's happened?

VI. He's alright. He was at a checkpoint. There was some sort of attack.

RHYS. What do you mean, some sort of attack?

VI. I don't know, they spoke so fast on the phone. It was one of those suicide bombers. Look, the two he was with, they've been killed.

RHYS. What happened?

VI. I don't know. He's fine. He's injured but he's fine.

RHYS. Jesus.

VI. He's in an army hospital in Basra. He's survived. They're keeping him in for two weeks and then . . .

RHYS. What?

VI. He's coming home, Rhys. He's coming home.

RHYS. Is he?

VI. It's a great day.

RHYS. A great day. And she'll be so happy.

VI. We all will be.

RHYS. Yes. So why the praying?

VI. Two of them are dead, Rhys. They've got mothers. I've been spared. Thank you God.

RHYS. Yes. Thank you God.

They pray.

VI. Rhys?

RHYS. Yes.

VI. Fancy a beer? I've got a six-pack in the fridge.

RHYS. No.

VI. I got that Garden-thingy, you know, the one you like. I got a lemon to go with it.

RHYS *gets up to leave.*

Where're you going?

RHYS. Out.

VI. Where out?

RHYS. Back up the hill, I should think.

VI. Don't go, Rhys.

RHYS. Why not?

VI. I want you to stay and I want you to know.

RHYS. What?

VI. I care for you.

RHYS. Do you?

VI. For both of you. You and Dai. I care for you equally.

RHYS. Oh yeah?

VI. I always have and I always will.

RHYS. That's funny because I'm a stupid shit.

RHYS *exits.*

VI. Bethan. Bethan.

BETHAN. What?

VI. Wake up!

BETHAN. What?

VI. I've got something to tell you.

BETHAN. What?

VI. It's Dai.

BETHAN. What?

VI. He's coming home.

BETHAN. What?

VI. There's been an accident. He's been injured but only slightly. He's coming home!

BETHAN. Injured?

VI. I spoke to his Sergeant, you know, the one from Swansea. He's fine. He's having a checkup, that's all.

BETHAN. He's alright?

VI. Yes.

BETHAN. Have you spoken to him?

VI. No. He's in hospital. They're just keeping him under observation. He's fine. He'll be home in two weeks.

BETHAN. Two weeks!

VI. It's a great day, Bethan. It's a great day!

BETHAN. Fourteen days!

VI. Here in this house. In this room. Standing.

BETHAN. Thank you.

VI. I know.

BETHAN. Oh God, oh God, oh God.

VI. Yes.

BETHAN. Are you sure?

VI. Of course I'm sure. I need a drink.

> VI *gets two bottles of beer and opens the first one. She offers it to* BETHAN.

Here, it's a Garden-thingy.

BETHAN. No thanks.

> VI *holds up the bottle.*

VI. To the future.

> BETHAN *takes the bottle and sips.*

BETHAN. The future.

VI. Bloody incredible.

BETHAN. Yes.

VI. Hungry?

BETHAN. No.

VI. Toast?

BETHAN. I'm fine.

VI. You have to have something. Life carries on, Bethan.

BETHAN. Alright.

> VI *makes toast.* DAI *enters the kitchen dressed in perfect white pyjamas with his arm in a sling and one of his legs in a plaster.*

DAI. Bethan!

BETHAN. Dai!

DAI. Bethan! I'm home. I love you!

BETHAN. And I love you!

DAI. I've missed you so much.

BETHAN. I've missed you so much!

DAI. The helicopter dropped me off.

BETHAN. Just like you said it would. I saw the pilot. I waved! Did they drop you at the top of the hill? Your arm. Does it hurt?

DAI. It's fine. It'll be better soon. Look.

He moves his arm.

BETHAN. You're so brave!

DAI. Will you marry me? Say yes! Say yes, you'll marry me!

BETHAN. Yes! Oh Yes!

DAI. Let me hold you!

BETHAN. Tight! Hold me tight!

DAI. Tight!

They kiss.

You're beautiful.

BETHAN. Make love to me.

DAI. Yes, let's make love. Now. Here.

VI *brings in the toast.*

VI. Here you go. It's just got butter on.

BETHAN. Thanks.

VI. I love toast. I don't know why and I know it's not that good for you but I just do. It's so warm and crunchy and comforting. It's perfect.

BETHAN. I like toast too.

VI. It's so soothing. You know, Bethan, I love the world. I do. I love it. I love life. I love this moment. Here. Now. It exists.

BETHAN. Got any more butter?

VI. On the side. Listen.

She plays 'Wild Horses' by the Rolling Stones.

What do you think?

BETHAN. I like it.

VI. I love the Stones.

>VI *raises her hands to the ceiling as the music swells.*

>Gwilym! Gwilym! Gwilym! Dai's home! Thank you. Thank you.

>VI *imagines* DAI*'s return.*

DAI. Mother.

VI. Dai!

DAI. I'm here.

VI. Dai.

DAI. I'm back.

VI. Dai!

DAI. I'm home.

VI. Let me hold you.

DAI. Hold me tight.

VI. Tight.

>*She holds him and cries.*

>Dai.

DAI. That's me.

VI. My son.

DAI. They read me the last rites. Got the Chaplain in and he's standing next to the bed droning on, may Almighty God release you from all punishments in this life, and I thought you can forget that for a lark cos I'm not dead yet and I've got things to do!

VI. They read you the last rites?

DAI. Yeah.

VI. But you're not a Catholic.

DAI. There was a cock-up. You look terrible. Been alright?

VI. Yes. No. I don't know. I'm not sure. It's difficult to judge.
Sometimes it's fine, at others it's . . . fragile. You know?
Fragile. Oh Dai!

DAI. I'm here, aren't I?

VI. I thought of you everyday.

DAI. You can stop the tears.

VI. I put a quiet time aside every morning here, at this table.
I summoned you up in incredible detail so I could hold your
face in my mind.

DAI. You look beautiful, Mother. Beautiful.

VI. And now you're here.

DAI. I'm a bit different now.

VI. I'm so sorry.

DAI. You told the others then?

VI. They know a bit. I didn't want to worry them.

DAI. That was the right thing to do.

VI. You said to keep it secret.

DAI. I did. The doctors say I'll get better. She'll scream when
she sees me.

VI. No, she won't. She doesn't care how you come back as
long as she has you.

DAI. She been seeing Rhys?

VI. Everything's fine.

DAI. You sure?

VI. They're friends.

DAI. I'll go now if they've been sleeping with each other.

VI. They don't see each other much, I can assure you of that.
Look at her.

DAI. She been eating?

VI. Only toast.

DAI. What's been the matter?

VI. You.

DAI. Me?

VI. She longs for you.

DAI. I'd forgotten her face.

VI. She often comes. She wants to be near you.

DAI. I'd forgotten her. I'd bloody forgotten her.

VI. Go on. Speak to her.

DAI. Bethan.

BETHAN. Dai! Oh Dai! Oh David. Oh David Aubrey
Williams. It's you! It's you! Your sweet face! I love you!
I love you! Please. I fainted. I saw you, the helicopter! It
circled. It went round the hill. I love you so much. I've
missed you so much . . . Oh God, please, I love you. Kiss
me! Now! Kiss me! Kiss me! Please! Now! Now! Please.
Please. Kiss me!

VI. I told you everything would be alright.

Scene Seven

Rhys imagines Dai returning

The top of the hill.

RHYS *is standing.* DAI *enters.*

RHYS. You're back.

DAI. Yeah.

RHYS. You alright?

DAI. Tremendous.

RHYS. I was worried.

DAI. Me too.

Scene Eight

Dai returns

The kitchen.

RHYS *is decorating a banner saying* 'WELCOME HOME DAI'.
BETHAN *enters.*

RHYS. About time. Where've you been?

BETHAN. Finishing this.

RHYS. What took you? I've been struggling.

BETHAN. What do you think?

She shows a cake with 'WELCOME HOME DAI' *on it.*

RHYS. That's nice, that is.

BETHAN. Took me ages.

RHYS. Let's have a taste.

BETHAN. Get your hands off, will you!

RHYS. He's not going to eat it all, is he?

BETHAN. Maybe he will. Just leave it alone.

RHYS. Kiss me.

BETHAN. Leave off, will you.

BETHAN *hands* RHYS *some balloons.*

Blow these up, will you. You've got enough hot air in there.

RHYS. Yeah, yeah.

BETHAN. If we'd got a bouncy castle, you'd have had that up
in five minutes, the rubbish you talk.

RHYS. Do you want these done then?

BETHAN. Just saying.

RHYS. I'd like to bounce you on one of those castles.

VI enters.

VI. Never mind bouncing on castles, put some suitable music on, will you.

RHYS *puts on some music. It's loud.*

I said suitable music, not that tuneless rubbish.

RHYS *plays different music.*

Please!

RHYS. What?

VI. You know what.

RHYS. I thought you'd like it.

VI. You know what thought did.

RHYS. Yes, yes.

VI. Just put something suitable on, will you! Try and use the intelligence God gave you.

RHYS. It's my favourite music. It's totally, utterly suitable.

VI. And there's no need for that swearing.

RHYS. I didn't swear.

VI. Don't answer back.

RHYS. I didn't swear.

VI. You'd test the patience of a saint, you would. Put something on.

He changes the music.

Very funny.

BETHAN. It's one extreme to another. What's a matter with your taste?

RHYS. I've got good taste in everything.

BETHAN. In some things you have.

RHYS. You put something on then.

BETHAN *selects a CD.*

That's pathetic.

VI. What did I say about swearing?

RHYS. I didn't swear.

VI. Try something else, Bethan.

BETHAN *selects another CD.*

Oh he'll like that. Tuneful, innit? He can dance to that, can't
he? We could all dance to that, it's got a rhythm.

The music plays. BETHAN, RHYS *and* VI *dance.*

DAI *enters in a wheelchair paralysed down his left side, he
cannot speak properly. They stop dancing.*

Turn it off.

DAI. Home.

No one moves.

Hold me!

No one moves.

Hold me.

No one moves.

Tight. Hold me. Tight.

No one moves.

BETHAN. Jesus.

RHYS. I thought he'd injured his arm.

DAI. Tight.

BETHAN. What's he saying?

VI. I'm going to hold him, I want to hold him.

She doesn't move.

DAI. Touch me.

BETHAN. I can't understand what you're saying.

RHYS. I told you.

VI. My poor, poor boy.

BETHAN. I'm going to be sick.

RHYS. Bloody hell.

DAI. Walk. I. Can. Walk.

DAI *stands up and then collapses.*

RHYS *(sings)*.
Mae hen whlad fy nhadau yn anwyl i mi,
Gwlad beirdd a chantorion, enwogion o fri;
Ei gwol rhyfeklwyr, gwlad garwyr tra mad,
Tros ryddid colladant eu gwaed.

Gwlad, gwlad, pleidiol wyf i'm gwlad,
Tra mor yn fur
I'r bur hoff bau,
O bydded i'r heniaith barhau.

Scene Nine

Rhys remembers the tossing of the coins (2)

By the river.

DAI. How many's that?

RHYS. Seven.

DAI. You sure?

RHYS. Yes.

DAI. This is serious, you know.

RHYS. You think I don't know that?

DAI. Seven then.

RHYS. Five for you. Two for me.

DAI. That's right.

RHYS. For eight then.

DAI. For eight.

RHYS. Heads.

DAI. Tails. You lose. That's six for me and two for you. Yes?

RHYS. Yes.

DAI. Things aren't looking so good for you.

Scene Ten

Rhys helps Vi

The kitchen.

Late at night.

DAI *is asleep on the sofa.* VI *is asleep at the table surrounded by leaflets, cards, envelopes and boxes of letters.* RHYS *enters.*

RHYS. You know what time it is?

VI. No, I don't.

RHYS. It's gone two o'clock. You must get to bed.

VI. How can I rest?

RHYS. You must try.

VI. My poor Dai. My poor, poor boy. You saw his face.

RHYS. I saw everything about him.

VI. What's going to happen?

RHYS. God knows. We'll be no use to him if we're exhausted.

   VI *starts to pack the envelopes.*

   Will you leave those alone?

VI. I have to finish them for tomorrow.

RHYS. Why?

VI. They collect on Thursdays. I'm totally behind.

RHYS. It's too much. You'll have to stop.

VI. We need the money.

RHYS. Mother, you must sleep.

VI. I've got these to do.

RHYS. For crying out loud . . .

VI. Go back to bed.

RHYS. We can't go on like this, not with Dai as he is.

VI. Like what?

RHYS. Let's be realistic for a change.

VI. What do you mean?

RHYS. We'll have to sell.

VI. I don't want to talk about it.

RHYS. Do you think I don't know about these?

   RHYS *opens a drawer stuffed full of bills. He shows them*
   to her.

   You know these can't be paid.

VI. Perhaps the bank'll give us more time.

RHYS. 'Lending stops eventually, Mr Williams.' That's what
   he said. He wasn't hostile.

VI. That's Bryan Davies that is, I knew him at school.

RHYS. Debt is debt.

VI. He kissed me once behind his dad's greenhouse.

RHYS. Bryan Davies?

VI. He held a torch for me.

RHYS. That'll change everything, that will.

VI. Well, you never know.

RHYS. Mother, be realistic.

VI. You saying I'm too old for that sort of thing?

RHYS. No. I'm just saying that's not how the banks operate.

VI. I know how men operate. He had terrible WHT.

RHYS. Terrible what?

VI. Wandering Hand Trouble. He was well known.

RHYS. Please. Spare me the details. Look, it's just not an option.

VI. I suppose not. It's all on computer now, isn't it?

RHYS. We're at the end. I've tried getting loans. No one will lend us any more money.

VI. Don't give up.

RHYS. I'm just saying.

VI. I wish we'd have caught Foot and Mouth.

RHYS. You don't.

VI. I do. Look at the Hamers. They got thousands of pounds in compensation.

RHYS. I detest them for it.

VI. No, they were clever, they paid for that lamb.

RHYS. I know that.

VI. They got it from that farm near Builth. One lamb condemned their whole flock. They got the market price in compensation. It was a master plan.

RHYS. Mother.

VI. We were clean. The Hamers put us in the three-mile radius. So we couldn't move anything, so we couldn't sell anything, so we're going bankrupt.

RHYS. I know.

VI. It's what killed your father.

RHYS. I know.

VI. It was the final straw.

RHYS. Mother, I know.

VI. The Hamers are cheats. Clean as whistles all those sheep were. And now I wish I'd done the same thing because my Gwilym would be here now.

RHYS. Yes.

VI. You're a good boy.

RHYS. Don't know about that. Shall we put all these bills away for now.

VI. Let's do that.

RHYS. We've managed for this long.

VI. Let's get them out the way.

They stuff the bills into the drawer.

RHYS. I'll help you finish these off.

He points to the cardboard boxes.

VI. Will you?

RHYS. We can do them together.

VI. Thank you.

RHYS. Bloody things.

They start stuffing the envelopes.

Scene Eleven

Dai spoils the envelopes

The kitchen.

DAI *wakes up suddenly from a nightmare. He finds his pills. He looks in a cup. It's empty. He struggles to the table to an open bottle of beer. He takes the pills and drinks the beer.*

The beer tips into a box of completed envelopes. He tears open some envelopes and scratches the cards.

Scene Twelve

After the reception

The kitchen.

VI *enters.*

Wedding presents are on the table.

RHYS *enters.*

VI. They'll be here in a minute.

RHYS. Coming.

VI. Can you get the champagne glasses?

RHYS. Champagne glasses? Since when did we have champagne glasses.

VI. Since yesterday, I bought some, didn't I? They're in the front room in a box marked 'Flutes'.

RHYS. Flutes?

VI. It's what they're called.

RHYS. You bought flutes?

VI. What was I meant to do?

RHYS. After everything we said about money.

VI. Not now.

RHYS. You know he's not allowed to drink.

VI. He can have a ginger beer.

RHYS. I do wonder about you, Mother.

VI. Please get them.

>RHYS *goes to get them.*

>The church was packed, wasn't it? And not a dry eye in the house. She looked beautiful. Radiant. The reception's going well, people are enjoying themselves. And he survived it.

RHYS. Everyone's rallying round.

VI. Life turns funny corners.

RHYS. Life's a fricking banana.

>RHYS *returns with the glasses.*

VI. How many times do I have to say don't swear? It drives me mad.

RHYS. Fricking's not swearing.

VI. It's as good as swearing.

RHYS. Mother!

VI. Just you watch your fricking. I'll go back down to the hall in a bit after they've settled in here. Maybe have a dance. He looked so tired and so happy.

>RHYS *lays out the champagne flutes. A car draws up.*

>Quick. They're here. Ginger Beer.

>*The sound of doors opening and the wheelchair being unloaded.* BETHAN *enters dressed as a bride.*

BETHAN. Give me a hand to get him through the door.

RHYS. Let's have a look.

>*He looks at* BETHAN's *wedding ring and tries to kiss it.*

BETHAN. Don't do that.

RHYS. I wish you luck.

BETHAN. Just give me a hand, will you?

VI. Is everything OK?

DAI (*calling from outside*). Bethan!

BETHAN. Coming!

DAI. Bethan!

BETHAN. I'm coming. Not now, alright? Not now, just help.
    Can you give me a hand to get him in?

RHYS. Of course.

> BETHAN *and* RHYS *exit.* VI *puts music on: 'Here Comes
> the Bride'.* RHYS *pushes the chair into the room.* BETHAN
> *is sitting on* DAI's *lap.*

> She's being carried across the threshold.

DAI. Kiss me.

BETHAN. Later. Handsome man.

> VI *opens the champagne and a bottle of ginger beer.*

VI. Champagne!

RHYS. I'll pour.

VI. To the happy couple!

RHYS. To the future!

VI. Dai and Bethan Williams.

RHYS. You got a good one there.

DAI. Yes.

VI. You're a beautiful girl, Bethan.

BETHAN. Thank you. Thank you.

VI. So you're a farmer's wife now.

BETHAN. And a soldier's.

VI. Can't be bad.

RHYS. Top up, everyone?

VI. Top everyone up, that's right. You're a good one, Rhys.

RHYS. You talking about me?

VI. You heard. He only says that to try and make me repeat it.

DAI. Rhys.

BETHAN. To Rhys!

RHYS. To the happy couple.

VI. We've said that.

RHYS. I know. I wanted to do it as well.

VI. Go on then.

RHYS. To the happy couple.

VI. Rhys. We're going back now to the church hall, so we can see off the last of the guests.

RHYS. I've only just started my champagne.

VI. Never mind that. Come on.

RHYS. Just wait, will you!

VI. They've just married.

   VI *points to the door.*

RHYS. Of course. Sorry. Yes.

   RHYS *and* VI *exit.*

DAI. You married me!

BETHAN. What?

DAI. You married me!

BETHAN. Yes, I married you.

DAI. I'll get better.

BETHAN. You're in a chair.

DAI. Ambush.

BETHAN. What?

DAI. Blown up.

BETHAN. I can't understand you.

DAI. We're home.

BETHAN. We're home?

DAI. Came, up, lane.

BETHAN. Come up lane? Are you saying 'lane'?

DAI. Yes.

BETHAN. I thought you'd injured your arm.

DAI. Look. At me.

BETHAN. Your arm's OK.

DAI. Ambush.

BETHAN. Ambush. Ambush. Ambush. I know.

DAI. Hold me.

BETHAN. Yes.

She does not move.

DAI. Tight.

BETHAN. Yes.

She does not move.

DAI. Please.

BETHAN. Yes.

She does not move.

DAI. You must.

BETHAN. I'm going to.

DAI. I love you.

BETHAN. I'm going to kill whoever did this to you.

DAI. Help me.

BETHAN. Yes, I'll help you.

DAI. I'll get better.

BETHAN. I'm going to kiss you now.

DAI. Thank you.

    BETHAN *is sick.*

BETHAN. I'm sorry. It's the excitement.

DAI. What can I do?

BETHAN. I'm so sorry.

DAI. Your eyes. They're like the sea. They're beautiful.

    BETHAN *gets up and exits to get a cloth to clear up the sick.* DAI *slides out of the chair and beats his head gently on the floor.* BETHAN *returns.*

BETHAN. Stop it.

DAI. I want to.

BETHAN. Stop it. Get up.

DAI. I like it.

BETHAN. Please.

    He carries on banging his head.

DAI. You. People. Like. Me. Hospital. You. Look. After. Them.

BETHAN. I pity them.

DAI. Stay.

BETHAN. Don't do this.

DAI. Kiss me.

BETHAN. I can't.

DAI. Take your top off.

    She undoes her top.

BETHAN. Like this?

DAI. Yes. More.

BETHAN. No.

DAI. I want you.

BETHAN. For God's sake.

DAI. I'll crawl.

BETHAN. What for?

DAI *crawls.*

DAI. I'm crawling for you.

BETHAN. Stop it.

DAI. Look after me. Beautiful.

BETHAN. Stop it. Get up. I don't like it.

DAI. I love you.

BETHAN. Don't say those words.

DAI. Fuck me. I want. You. Fuck me. Let me. Fuck you. Let me. Cock's hard. My princess. I lay in the mud. Thought of you. Kept me alive.

DAI *crawls.* BETHAN *hits him.*

BETHAN. Idiot.

DAI. Princess.

BETHAN. You stupid, stupid . . .

DAI. My beloved.

BETHAN *faces* DAI.

BETHAN. Dai. Look at me. Are you looking? Can you see all of me?

DAI. Yes.

BETHAN *takes off her top.*

BETHAN. Look. Do you like what you see?

DAI. Yes.

BETHAN *slowly undresses to her bra.*

Beautiful.

BETHAN. Let me kiss you.

BETHAN *kisses him. She caresses him.* DAI *comes.*

DAI. Oh. Sorry.

BETHAN. Oh my God.

DAI. Sorry.

BETHAN. It's nothing.

DAI. I sorry.

BETHAN. It's all over the dress.

DAI. Never. Mind.

BETHAN. It's hired you know, it has to go back tomorrow.

DAI. Sorry.

BETHAN. It's nothing.

DAI. Sorry.

BETHAN. Don't worry. I'm flattered.

DAI. I do.

BETHAN. I said it's nothing.

BETHAN *gets dressed and exits.*

Scene Thirteen

Stones

The kitchen.

VI *is sitting at the table surrounded by the remains of the food. She pulls stones out of the cake tin and places them on the table next to a ball of string.*

VI. Stones with holes in. This is what you liked to collect. They give you good luck, you said. I never thought.

She holds a stone up to the light.

I miss your hands on me. And your weight. Pressing. On me, like you used to.

I thought you loved me. But you must have hated me. Did the river call you? This one's a nice smooth one. Was it curiosity? Did the currents pull you in? Draw you on? What did you have to know for?

She threads string through the hole in another stone.

You were tethered, yes, to Llanelwedd, but you could have waited, seen things through. What about responsibility?

She holds up her hand and takes off her wedding ring.

The fattest one in the shop. I wondered when it would be time for you to go. Let's have a good look then. Still beautiful.

She ties the stone and puts it around her neck.

Where are you now? Floating, free, weightless.

She picks up phone and dials.

Could I speak to Paul Hutchison, please? Yes, it's Vi Williams from Llanelwedd Farm.

Scene Fourteen

The rejection

Beside a river.

Evening.

RHYS. What do you want?

BETHAN. I want to see you.

RHYS. Do you now?

BETHAN. Haven't seen you for a while.

RHYS. Been keeping away.

BETHAN. You shouldn't do that.

RHYS. With what you've done to him?

BETHAN. Keeping away from me's no good.

RHYS. I want to. My poor brother. You're humiliating him. One minute, you're married; the next, not even there. Why?

BETHAN. Vi's not speaking to me.

RHYS. So.

BETHAN. I tried.

RHYS. Did you?

BETHAN. Missed you.

RHYS. It's only been a couple of days.

BETHAN. Rhys.

RHYS. Go away.

BETHAN. I want to talk.

RHYS. Sure you do.

BETHAN. My man.

RHYS. Your man's at home.

BETHAN. I mean it.

RHYS. Don't confuse me.

BETHAN. I've been sick.

RHYS. So.

BETHAN. I've been stupid.

RHYS. Don't go on.

BETHAN. I waited for him and now he's back and I've tried but I can't. Surely you can see that. It's you. I love you. I want you, you know that.

RHYS. Buzzard hovering over there.

BETHAN. Put your hand on my head.

RHYS. Look at the bugger. Beautiful. Got his eye on something, I should think. I won't be doing that any more.

BETHAN. I need peace.

RHYS. Incredible how they stay in one place. In the air. Subtle.

BETHAN. Please.

RHYS. You had your chance.

BETHAN. God.

RHYS. He's my brother.

BETHAN. As soon as I saw him, I knew it was you I needed. It's not his injury. It's you.

RHYS. Too late.

BETHAN. Isn't.

RHYS. He's ruined.

BETHAN. I think about you all the time.

RHYS. I'm going to look after him. Make sure he's alright. I'm going to extend the house, build him facilities. Somewhere decent. So that he can live.

BETHAN. Come away with me.

RHYS. The poor bugger can't speak properly. I'm not going anywhere.

BETHAN. I imagine you coming to my house. I'm asleep. You call me, I wake, come down the stairs, rub my eyes, get in the car and we drive. Through the night to the coast. We watch the dawn rising, sun on the sea. Sit together, waves crash, holding hands. It's all I want.

RHYS. It's too late.

BETHAN. Kiss me.

RHYS. No.

BETHAN. Please.

RHYS. I can't.

BETHAN. I kiss so gently. Surely you remember?

RHYS. I mustn't.

BETHAN. Hold me.

RHYS. No.

BETHAN. Just for a minute.

RHYS. Leave me alone.

BETHAN. It's alright.

RHYS. I can't sleep any more. I wake in the night covered in sweat. I toss and turn. My tongue sticks to the roof of my mouth.

BETHAN. I'm not strong enough to look after him.

RHYS. He needs me.

BETHAN. Come with me.

RHYS. It's over.

BETHAN. No.

RHYS. He needs us, he's desperate. It's what I want. And so should you.

BETHAN. I can't.

RHYS. It's your duty.

BETHAN. Duty to who?

RHYS. Don't be selfish.

BETHAN. What?

RHYS. You know what you have to do and so do I.

BETHAN. You can't control me.

RHYS. It's what's right.

BETHAN. You can't be my conscience. I am me. We're different. Kiss me.

RHYS. No way.

BETHAN. Don't hate me. Kiss me.

RHYS. Kiss you?

The sound of a Chinook in the distance.

RHYS. You can hang out the back of them, you know?

BETHAN. What?

RHYS. Chinooks have two main rotor blades. They make a bubble of air at the back.

BETHAN. Do they?

RHYS. It's a vacuum.

BETHAN. So?

RHYS. You can get into it.

BETHAN. What do you mean?

RHYS. You attach a harness and you get into it and you fly.

BETHAN. Fly? Who told you that?

RHYS. One of the pilots I met down the Llanerch. You go weightless, it's like you're on the moon.

BETHAN. That's it. It's that. I want it.

RHYS. I'll ask him if you can go.

BETHAN. Would you?

RHYS. Yes.

BETHAN. Kiss me.

RHYS. No.

They kiss.

Scene Fifteen

Rhys remembers the tossing of the coin (3)

By the river.

DAI. Ready?

RHYS. Heads. Heads.

   DAI *tosses the coin.*

DAI. Heads it is.

RHYS. Let me look.

   RHYS *looks.*

   That's six to you and four to me. Agreed?

DAI. Yes. Again. You this time.

   He hands RHYS *the coin.*

RHYS. Heads or tails?

DAI. Heads.

   RHYS *tosses the coin.*

RHYS. Heads it is.

DAI. Seven to me, four to you. So this is possibly the last one?

RHYS. What do you mean?

DAI. Best of fifteen is the same as the first to eight.

RHYS. I know that. I'll toss. Heads or tails?

DAI. I know that.

RHYS. What.

DAI. Heads or tails? It's bound to be, isn't it?

RHYS. Yes.

DAI. So why do you keep asking me?

RHYS. Don't know.

DAI. You've asked me enough. Let's do this one in silence.

RHYS. If it pleases you.

RHYS *tosses the coin.*

DAI. Heads.

RHYS. Heads it is.

DAI. You know what that means?

RHYS. Yes.

DAI. You.

RHYS. Yes. You stay. I go.

DAI. Yes. You go, I stay. Fuck, I'm crying.

RHYS. I'm fine.

DAI. Fuck. Fuck. Fuck. Fuck. Fuck. I can't say it. I've never said it.

RHYS. What?

DAI. Brother.

RHYS. What.

DAI. I.

RHYS. Yeah.

DAI. You know.

RHYS. Yeah.

DAI. I fucking . . .

RHYS. I know.

Scene Sixteen

Hospital Two

The patient hasn't moved. BETHAN enters with flowers.

BETHAN. I bought you these. Couldn't resist them. They're so
    pretty. I saw Geraint with Myra today. She's got new
    trainers and Geraint, well, I don't know what he wears. He's
    got the weirdest dress sense ever. Orange looks terrible on
    him. And Myra doesn't do her moustache which is
    headstrong. You know they think you might be the enemy.
    There's no matching DNA profile. We picked you up by
    mistake. It happens. You're an Iraqi.

Scene Seventeen

The picnic

The top of the hill.

RHYS *has carried* DAI *up the hill.*

RHYS. Bloody knackered.

DAI. Thanks. Carry.

RHYS. Taken me an hour.

   He puts him down. DAI *looks at the view.*

DAI. Fences. Bad.

RHYS. Never mind.

DAI. Sheep. Look.

RHYS. Bloody sheep'll get through anything. They're clever
    beggars when it comes to gaps. You remember that?

DAI. Wander.

RHYS. What?

DAI. Wander.

RHYS. They wander alright. Can't control the rascally creatures.

DAI. Fix them.

RHYS. In due course.

DAI. Father.

RHYS. Yes, Father would have.

DAI. Grave.

RHYS. His grave? It looks fine, I'll take you there. Bethan planted some forget-me-nots. Another time, alright? I'm sorry.

DAI. Why?

RHYS. I'm sorry that you went. To the war.

DAI. Army's brilliant.

RHYS. Is it?

DAI. Fucked so much. Blow jobs. All the time. Lovely. Soft gentle cunts.

RHYS. Did you?

DAI. All the time. Surprised?

RHYS. Yes.

DAI. Me too.

RHYS. You just said . . .

DAI. That's there . . .

RHYS. Yes but . . .

DAI. Different.

RHYS. Is it?

DAI. War. No rules.

RHYS. Bloody hell.

DAI. Jealous?

RHYS. Yes. Listen.

> RHYS *takes an old bicycle bell and rings it.*

DAI. Father's.

RHYS. Remember two boys on a bicycle crossbar, down Shakey Bridge hill?

DAI. Yes.

RHYS. It's how I remember him, the three of us, air on my face, speeding down the hill.

DAI. Where?

RHYS. The bike? I used the frame to patch up that hole in the hedge over there. The back wheel's over there. The front's there. See. Filled them up nicely.

DAI. Wrecked.

RHYS. He's gone, Dai. He's not here any more.

DAI. Topped himself.

RHYS. No one's sure.

DAI. I am.

RHYS. You can't be.

DAI. Yes.

RHYS. No, no one'll ever be sure exactly what happened.

DAI. Bethan?

RHYS. What about her?

DAI. Kissed her?

RHYS. No, I haven't. I wouldn't do that, Dai. You can trust me.

DAI. Fuck?

RHYS. No! I haven't touched her. I don't want to touch her. And I certainly haven't fucked her. I don't even see her much.

DAI. Have.

RHYS. I'm not interested.

DAI. Have.

RHYS. What?

DAI. I'll.

RHYS. Yes.

DAI. I'll.

RHYS. You can't do anything now.

DAI. Can.

RHYS. I'm your brother, not the enemy.

   VI *arrives.*

VI. Boys. Boys.

DAI. Mother.

RHYS. Mother.

DAI. Waiting.

VI. I know you have. Not to worry. Don't normally come up
   here during the morning, suppose because it's on the
   doorstep. It's beautiful, you must have missed this, Dai?

DAI. Yeah.

VI. It's a dream come true seeing you there and both looking
   so handsome!

DAI. Tell?

RHYS. Dai was saying the fences don't look too good.

DAI. Rubbish farmer.

RHYS. Too many gaps. Half the animals will be out if we're
   not careful, he's been saying. Chatting away about all sorts
   haven't you, Dai?

DAI. No.

RHYS. Please yourself.

VI. This is what I dreamed of. The three of us up here. In the sun.

They stare into the distance.

Paul Hutchison's just left. He came with the London woman.

RHYS. What?

VI. He could have starred in *Jaws*, that boy.

RHYS. You said you'd never talk to him again.

VI. If we sell now we can leave with some money. If we carry on, there'll be nothing left except debt. If we leave the farm in August, we'll be alright. They still want it. They've got kids.

DAI. Want. Stay.

VI. I want to. But we can't. We'll move into the town. When I said the farm lost money every year, Joanna, that's her name, she just smiled and she said that she didn't think it would be a problem. They've got no idea about farming. They're going to do up the house and visit at weekends. She's a pleasant woman.

They're quiet.

Help me spread this out, can you?

VI lays out a tablecloth and puts out a cake tin. She opens it and takes out a cake. She divides it up.

Eat.

They eat.

RHYS. I don't know what I'll do.

DAI. Me. Neither.

RHYS. Work in one of those coffee shops, I suppose.

VI. I told Joanna, the farm will need a manager.

RHYS. Me? No. I don't think I could do that. That wouldn't be correct. No.

The Chinook approaches. DAI *trembles.*

VI. You're trembling. Bad memories?

DAI. Yes.

The Chinook passes over.

Don't like. Don't like.

VI. You'll be alright. Let it out.

DAI. Hate. It.

VI. Just let it out!

DAI *struggles to get up. He writhes, managing a strange dance.*

DAI. You. You bastards.

VI. That's it. Use army language if it helps.

DAI. You. Fucking. Fuck-pig bastards. You. Wanking. Fucking. Fuck-pig cunts. I fucking hate you! I fucking. Loathe you. You rat-arsed, vermin-shaped creeps. I fucking loathe you. Arse pigs. Motherfucking. Piss-taking dogs. You fucking tarts! You fucking twelve-headed trollops. You stinking fucking arse-licking wretches. I hate you. The things I have seen. You fuckers! The things I have seen! It doesn't go away! The things I have seen! It doesn't go away!

VI. Let me hold you.

DAI. Fuck-pig slut.

VI. Let me.

DAI. Shit-faces.

RHYS. Stop it!

DAI. Arse fuck cunt.

VI. Please stop.

DAI. Arse fuck cunt.

VI. Help me.

RHYS. Stop it!

DAI. Bitch.

They all hold onto DAI *as he tears at his body.*

VI. Please.

DAI. Bethan!

Scene Eighteen

Vi sings

The kitchen.

VI (*sings*).
   Abide with me; fast falls the eventide,
   The darkness deepens: Lord with me abide.
   When other helpers fail and comforts flee,
   Help of the helpless, O abide with me.

   Swift to its close ebbs out life's little day;
   Earth's joys grow dim; its glories pass away;
   Change and decay in all around I see;
   O Thou who changest not abide with me.

Scene Nineteen

Dai cannot speak

The kitchen.

Evening.

DAI *is shivering uncontrollably.*

VI. There's an ambulance on the way. The paramedic will be
   here first, on a motorbike. They say fifteen minutes.

DAI. Good.

VI. That's what they say.

DAI. Yes.

VI. It's the soonest they could make it. They'll give you some help. Medical profession. Saints, really.

DAI. Yes.

VI. Sometimes things just happen and there's nothing you can do about them but they alter you.

DAI. Yeah.

VI. Everything adds up.

DAI. Yeah.

VI. Suddenly you've been spoilt. The you of you's gone. You're someone else.

DAI. Yes.

VI. Did you kill people in Iraq?

DAI. Yes.

VI. Does it haunt you?

DAI. Yeah.

VI. I suppose it was you or them.

DAI. Yeah.

VI. If the crowds moved towards you, you shot at them.

DAI. Yes.

VI. Women, children. It was the only thing you could do. Afterwards, you saw their bodies swelling in the sun. There they are. No one, really. Just in the way.

DAI. Yes.

VI. You've seen things no one should see; done things no one should do?

DAI. True.

VI. I sent you.

VI *prays.*

Dear God. I ask for your mercy. In my hour of need. I ask for your forgiveness. I do not presume to come to your table. We are not worthy so much as to gather crumbs . . .

DAI. Don't.   ·

VI. I must.

DAI. Faces. Faces.

VI. Faces?

DAI. Screaming.

VI. Screaming?

DAI. Cold. Cold.

She wraps them both up in a blanket.

VI. Why did I do nothing?

DAI. Nothing to do.

VI. I'll get Rhys to fix the bike tomorrow. Cycle down Castle Hill.

DAI. Castle Hill.

VI. We'll have a picnic at the river.

DAI. Cake. Like before.

VI. Yes.

DAI. Mother?

VI. Yes.

DAI. I'm frightened.

VI. Let me hold you. Hold me.

DAI. Frightened. Quiet.

VI. Help's on its way.

DAI. I remember everything.

VI. You'll be alright.

DAI. All of it.

VI. I'll look after you. We'll catch a fish in the river. We'll throw stones in the water. We'll drink tea on the green rug.

DAI. Good things.

DAI *falls asleep.*

VI. Yeah, good things. That's it, Dai, that's it.

DAI *has a nightmare. He wakes and stands up.*

DAI. Mother! Faces!

VI. Quiet.

DAI. Can't.

VI. Sleep.

DAI. Can't.

VI. Can.

DAI. Won't.

VI. Will.

DAI. Silence. I want silence.

VI. They'll be here soon.

DAI *hands* VI *a pillow.*

DAI. Smother me.

VI *refuses it.*

Smother me.

VI. No.

DAI. Smother me.

VI. I can't.

DAI. You can.

DAI *holds out the pillow.* VI *accepts it.*

Thank you.

She smothers him. He struggles vehemently. She stops.

Again.

VI. I can't.

DAI. Please. Before. They. Come.

VI. No.

DAI. I beg you.

VI. I can't. I won't. No. No. I'm sorry.

RHYS *enters.*

RHYS. Mother.

Scene Twenty

Hospital Three

BETHAN *attends the patient.*

BETHAN. I'm going to turn you off now. While Myra's out. You'll hear a horrible sharp sound, that's the ventilator alarm. But then you'll have quiet and the alarm for the heart monitor will sound but you won't hear that. You'll have peace by then.

BETHAN *turns off the ventilator.*

Scene Twenty-One

Leaving the farm

The kitchen.

Everything has been cleared out. VI is dressed in black, holding the cake tin full of stones. BETHAN looks out of the window.

BETHAN. All this eviction rubbish. It's unnecessary. London buyers. Paul Hutchison. Joanna. Hot air. It's not your fault. No one blames you. It's a quirk of history. Maybe you'll like the city. More faces there. More things to do. The flat's quite near a park. There's some nice little walks. We'll see what's what. Don't be nervous, it'll be fine. Come on, Vi. We have to go now.

BETHAN *exits.* VI *empties the cake tin onto the floor.*

It's full of stones.

Scene Twenty-Two

Cardiff

A small, shabby flat in Cardiff.

Day.

Noise of traffic. Curtains drawn.

VI *sits in a corner, unable to speak. She holds a stone.* BETHAN *stands.* RHYS *enters.*

BETHAN. Rhys.

RHYS. Hello, Bethan.

BETHAN. You well?

RHYS. Fair to poxy.

BETHAN. You look well. Tired but well.

RHYS. A lot's been happening, you know how it is, all these things, do you know? Tire you out a bit. Really. A lot. Sometimes. Drain you. You know. But you're alright, you're well?

BETHAN. I'm OK.

RHYS. I haven't been here for a while.

BETHAN. You don't visit much.

RHYS. No, it's . . . it's, you know, it's complicated. I get caught up.

BETHAN. Yes, it's busy.

RHYS. A big change with the farm going and everything. You know how it is.

BETHAN. Not really, no. I don't know.

RHYS. No, well.

BETHAN. Everything's different now.

RHYS. Yes, everything's different.

BETHAN. Mind, she's the same as ever.

RHYS. Still sits there like that, doing nothing?

BETHAN. Day in day out, all she ever does is clutch those bloody stones. Drives me mad. You talk to her.

RHYS. I will.

BETHAN. Go on.

RHYS. You've been so good to help her.

BETHAN. I don't see her that often.

RHYS. I appreciate it though, you're very kind, it's very kind of you.

BETHAN. You talk to her, see what happens, go on.

RHYS. Mother. Mother. We're worried about you.

BETHAN. She doesn't read. She doesn't talk.

RHYS. Mother. It's Rhys.

BETHAN. She often doesn't seem to move.

RHYS. You can't keep doing this.

BETHAN. She won't come out of it.

RHYS. You must pull yourself together.

BETHAN. She ignores everything.

RHYS. Mother. Stop this. For God's sake, stop it, will you? I'm your son. Remember?

RHYS *takes the stone out of* VI*'s hand. She resists.*

VI. Give it back to me.

RHYS. Why should I?

VI. It's mine.

RHYS. Talk to me.

VI. Why should I?

RHYS. You can't carry on like this.

VI. Why not?

RHYS. All this grief.

VI. Grief?

RHYS. You mustn't. You must move on. Everything moves on. Can't you see that I'm here?

VI. Give me back that stone.

RHYS. Come and get it.

VI. Here. Come. Here.

RHYS. You need help.

VI. Give it to me.

RHYS. I said come and get it.

VI. There's nothing.

RHYS. I'm your son.

VI. Nothing at all.

RHYS. I want to help you.

VI. I have nothing.

RHYS. The world doesn't stop.

VI. I am not here.

RHYS. There's just the two of us now, please, your grief, please stop.

VI. Grief holds me, bathes me, pulls me close, makes me whole. Grief's soft corners take me, cherish me. I rest my head on his lap. Do not ask me to give up my grief. It is my friend, my dark companion, my stone. Don't ask me to stop my grief, because I cannot.

RHYS. Mother, please.

VI. I can't.

RHYS. Let me hold your hand.

VI. I must keep it and you must go.

RHYS. Let me hold you. I think about you.

VI. Go, just go.

RHYS. Please.

   VI *closes her eyes.*

BETHAN. I'm sorry.

RHYS. It's not your fault.

BETHAN. You OK?

RHYS. Sometimes it's too much.

BETHAN. I know. You look handsome.

RHYS. Do I?

BETHAN. Yes, very. You do.

RHYS. You never said that before.

BETHAN. No. I was wondering?

RHYS. Yes.

BETHAN. One day, perhaps we could take a trip to the farm, together, look around. Maybe walk up the hill, sit on the top, take in the view perhaps?

RHYS. I don't know.

BETHAN. If you ever feel like it.

RHYS. Perhaps.

BETHAN. Maybe soon. I would like it so much. I would give anything for it.

RHYS. I'm not sure. I'm sorry. Life OK?

BETHAN. I work in town now. Gave up the nursing.

RHYS. Have you?

BETHAN. I wrote and told you.

RHYS. Did you?

BETHAN. I sent you a letter. I need to get away. Don't you?

RHYS. Yes.

BETHAN. Perhaps?

RHYS. I.

BETHAN. Yes?

RHYS. Nothing.

BETHAN. Please.

RHYS. What?

BETHAN. Remember. On the hill.

RHYS. Bethan, look, a lot's happened since then.

BETHAN. I often think about it.

RHYS. So do I.

BETHAN. So?

RHYS. It means so much to me.

BETHAN. It does to me too.

RHYS. I. My wife's in the car.

BETHAN. Your wife?

RHYS. She's waiting outside. She didn't want to meet you. Understandably.

BETHAN. Your wife?

RHYS. Yes, my wife.

BETHAN. Congratulations.

RHYS. I want to move on. I got you this.

BETHAN. What?

RHYS. It's the number of the Chinook pilot who might take you up. The vacuum bubble you can get into?

BETHAN. Thanks. I'll do that. I.

RHYS. I thought it might help.

BETHAN. I'll always . . .

RHYS. What?

BETHAN. You're married.

RHYS. Yes.

BETHAN. I.

RHYS. Me too.

BETHAN. Kiss me.

RHYS. I mustn't.

BETHAN. Just once. For the last time.

> RHYS *moves towards* BETHAN. *He is going to kiss her. She closes her eyes.*

BETHAN. Thank you. Just once.

RHYS. No.

> RHYS *exits.*

Scene Twenty-Three

Chinook

The back of a Chinook.

Flying.

BETHAN *is standing in the back of the Chinook. The noise is fierce. Over the Tannoy, we hear the* PILOT *shouting instructions.*

PILOT. Check your harness. The top and the bottom. If it breaks, we won't get you back. Top clip?

BETHAN *checks the top link and gives the OK signal.*

Bottom clip?

BETHAN *checks the bottom link and gives the OK signal.*

Counting down from ten: Ten, Nine, Eight, Seven, Six, Five, Four, Three, Two, One.

BETHAN *jumps and fights her way into the bubble.*

The noise of the Chinook fades to silence.

She dances.

She undoes her harness.

She's free.

BETHAN. I'm coming.

Blackout.

Notes

OPERATION TELIC. THREE DIVISIONS IN BASRA.

Approximately 480 soldiers from the First Battalion, the Royal Regiment of Wales, are employed in Operation Telic.

Hansard, 9 February 2004

Soldiers from the Royal Regiment of Wales are starting to return from their tour of duty in Iraq to their base in Germany. About 700 soldiers from the regiment have been stationed in the Gulf for six months and will begin to go back to their European barracks on Friday. Most of the work of the regiment, which recruits almost exclusively from Wales, involved maintaining law and order by constant patrolling . . .

On Wednesday, five soldiers from First Battalion, Royal Welch Fusiliers, were injured in blasts in Basra. The injured soldiers were being treated at local military hospitals in Basra.

BBC News Online, 23 April 2004